doll
Star

Create lots of ways to play onstage!

★ American Girl®

Published by American Girl Publishing
Copyright © 2012 by American Girl

Questions or comments? Call 1-800-845-0005,
visit **americangirl.com**, or write to Customer Service, American Girl,
8400 Fairway Place, Middleton, WI 53562-0497.

Printed in China
12 13 14 15 16 17 18 LEO 10 9 8 7 6 5 4 3 2 1

All American Girl marks are trademarks of American Girl.

Editorial Development: Trula Magruder

Art Direction & Design: Lisa Wilber

Production: Jeannette Bailey, Sarah Boecher, Judith Lary

Craft Stylist: Trula Magruder

Doll Stylist: Jane Amini

Set Stylist: Kim Sphar

Photography: Travis Mancl, Jeff Rockwell

Stock Photography: © iStockphoto/Rockard, © iStockphoto/xxmmxx,
© iStockphoto/eskymaks, © iStockphoto/jsemeniuk, © iStockphoto/AlesVeluscek,
© iStockphoto/duuuna, © iStockphoto/luoman, © iStockphoto/losw

Craft with Care

When creating crafts or accessories that will touch your doll, remember that dye colors from ribbons, felt, beads, and other supplies may bleed color onto a doll and leave permanent stains. To help prevent this, use light colors when possible, and check your doll often to make sure colors aren't transferring to her body or vinyl. And never get your doll wet! Water greatly increases the risk of dye rub-off.

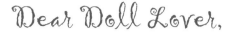

Dear Doll Lover,

Will your doll's road to fame lead to acting or directing? Cooking or writing? Singing or modeling? Will she be in the right place at the right time, or will she work hard until that one special opportunity arises? Will she go to auditions or will producers seek her out?

How will she handle talk shows and the press, or autograph signings and award shows? Will she change her name or use just her first name? Will you be her agent or a part of her entourage?

This book and the supplies inside will help your doll find the superstar career she's always dreamed of— but she'll need your help. So turn the page, and send your doll into stardom!

Your friends at American Girl

CRAFT WITH CARE!

Keep Your Doll Safe

When creating doll crafts, remember that dyes from ribbons, felt, beads, cords, fabrics, fleece, and other supplies may bleed onto your doll or her clothes and leave permanent stains. To help prevent this, use lighter colors when possible, and check your doll often to make sure the colors aren't transferring to her body, her vinyl, or her clothes. And never get your doll wet! Water and heat greatly increase dye rub-off.

It's Just Pretend

All the doll crafts in this book are for pretend only. So don't use hair-styling products or makeup on your doll, or try to plug in the pretend cords.

Get Help!

When you see this symbol 🖐 in the book, it means that you need an adult to help you with all or a part of the craft. Always ask for help before continuing.

Ask First

If a craft asks you to reuse an old item, such as a magazine or a piece of clothing, always ask an adult for permission before you use it. Your parent might still need it, so check first.

Craft Smart

If a craft instruction says "cut," use scissors. If it says "glue," use Glue Dots® or craft glue. And if it says "paint," use a nontoxic acrylic paint. Before you use these supplies, ask an adult to check them over—especially the paints and glues. Some crafting supplies are not safe for kids.

Put Away Crafts and Supplies

When you're not using the crafts or craft supplies, put them up high or store them away from little kids and pets. Toddlers and animals might eat your crafts, break them, or even hurt themselves when playing with them.

Search for Supplies

If you can't find an unusual or seasonal craft item (such as wood pieces or plastic treat canisters) at your local stores, ask an adult to check at scrapbook or craft stores or to search online. You can also see if a local store can order the supplies.

Rock Star

Give your doll a brilliant band, and let her rock the room!

Electric Guitars

Add power to your doll's performance with an electric guitar. For each guitar, punch out a body, neck, and face from the kit's glittery paper and card stock. Or look for your own favorite colors from a craft store. Attach the pieces as shown with Glue Dots. Draw guitar strings with a marker. Use the dots to add beads for control knobs, sequins for inlays, and ribbon for a strap.

Headset Microphone

Give your doll a hands-free mic. Cover a narrow straw with black duct tape, and glue a pom-pom to one end. Slip a hair elastic over her head, and slip in the straw.

Drums

Bring a beat to your doll's band with a drum set. For each drum, slip glitter paper inside plastic treat canisters, and use a Glue Dot to attach a shiny paper circle to the canister bottom. For legs, tightly wrap a rubber band around 3 unsharpened pencils. Stand the pencils on the erasers, and place a dot on each top. Slip a canister over the pencil tops. For a cymbal, put the eraser end of a pencil into a thread spool hole, and attach a canister lid to the other end with a dot. Add the kit's "Dolls Rock!" sticker to the front of a drum. Cut a narrow straw into drumsticks.

Amps

Help your doll's sound reach the back of the house with amplifiers. Wrap glitter paper around boxes, and seal closed with Glue Dots. Add paper circles for speakers, and connect a cord from each guitar to an amp with the dots. Decorate with white duct tape and beads.

Best Actress

Create a space for your doll to "take five" on her film sets.

Wardrobe Rack

Collect your doll's movie costumes on her personal rack. Cover two 12-inch-long dowels and one 18-inch-long dowel with silver duct tape, and connect the dowels with tape strips. Slip each dowel into the hole of a silver curling-ribbon tube. Hang up a few outfits.

Pro Makeup Kit

Keep a makeup kit ready for those between-scene touch-ups. Wrap craft boxes in shiny paper. Attach a small craft mirror with Glue Dots. Press the kit's blush and eyeshadow stickers to the box inserts. For a powder puff, use a dot to attach each end of a 3-inch ribbon to a cotton ball.

Hairstyling Center & Lighted Mirror

Keep a set stylist on standby! Place an old jewelry box on its side. Slip in empty mini lip-gloss tubes. For a hair dryer, cover empty glitter tubes with colored duct tape, and attach them with a Glue Dot. Tape on a cord. For a flat iron, wrap a hair elastic around 2 craft sticks. Add the kit's labels to the styling tools. For a wall mirror, use dots to attach white beads or plastic globe bulbs to a mini frame. Use shiny paper for the mirror.

9

Fashion Model

Dress your doll for strolls down the runway.

Runway

Create a professional catwalk for your doll to strut her styles. Use tape to hold 2 wooden crates (or cardboard boxes) side by side. Drape fabric over the crates, and attach glitter scrapbook paper along the tops with Glue Dots. Use the dots to attach the kit's fashion sign.

★ American Girl
FASHION
WEEK

Hip Hair

Now's the time to give your doll her most glamorous or unique hairstyle. Puff it up. Flatten it down. Add accessories. Have fun!

Mix & Match Outfits

Invite your friends and their dolls over for a fashion show. Mix and match doll clothes, or create your own fancy, crazy, or cool designs.

Show Singers

Invite your friends' dolls over for a singing and dancing extravaganza!

Show Costumes

Meet with your friends to create rows of performers. Dress your dolls in matching or similar clothing. Or, slip your doll into a leotard and tights. For a skirt, wrap a 12-inch fringe strip and a 12-inch ribbon around your doll's waist, and hold both together in back with a mini hair claw clip as shown at right. (Double the fringe if you can see through it.)

Fun Fascinator

For a chic hair accessory, cut an 8-inch netting square. Gather the netting in the middle, and attach it to the side of your doll's head with a girl-sized barrette as shown at right.

Show Set

To let each performer shine, place her on a riser. Use glue to stick foam board to craft wood. Or build risers from stacked CDs or cardboard boxes. Hang up the kit's choir sign to let other dolls know about the event.

Famed Director

Keep your doll focused on her film with just the right gear.

Headphones

Give your director earphones to hear her actors' sound recordings. To make a set, cover 2 wood dome disks with black duct tape. Slip a hair elastic on your doll's head like a headband. Attach the domes to each side of a second elastic with a Glue Dot. Slip that elastic on your doll's head and over her ears.

Director's Chair

Use a doll-sized canvas chair for a director's chair. Attach the kit's director label to the chair. Bring the chair along for location shoots, too.

Movie Camera

★ Ask an adult if you can turn an old plastic camera into a high-tech movie camera. To start, use Glue Dots to cover parts of the camera with black paper. Then add a penlight, a cliplight, or marker caps. For a stand, cover three 12-inch-long dowels, a 6-inch-long cardboard tube, and a 3-by-4-inch piece of craft wood with black duct tape. Tape the tube to the center of the wood. Wrap a rubber band around the top of the dowels, slip the tube over the top, and spread the dowels into a tripod. Balance the camera on the stand.

Action Essentials

To synchronize the sound with the start of the picture, pull out the kit's clapboard. Add the film's details with chalk. Roll the kit's megaphone into a cone. Use tape to seal it closed and to attach the handle. ID your director with the kit's studio badge. Tape a cord to the back top edges of the badge, and slip it over her neck.

15

Talk-Show Host

Show off your doll's personality on her daytime TV show.

Glamour Hair

Make a fancy accessory to match your doll's best outfit. Fan fold a 3-by-10-inch piece of **netting** (the fold should be 3 inches wide). Use a **Glue Dot** to fasten a short **ribbon** strip around the middle of the fan. Pull up the netting edges nearest the ribbon, and attach them together with a dot. Tie a matching ribbon around your doll's head, and add the bow to the ribbon with another dot.

Lapel Mic

Slip a length of **cord** through a **bead,** and tie a knot at one end. Drape the bead over the doll's shoulder to the front, leaving the remainder of the cord behind her back.

Show Set

Create a cozy set for your doll's talk show. Position doll chairs to face the movie camera from page 15. For a table, lay a large craft-wood circle on a craft box. Place a vase filled with flowers on the table. Attach each of the kit's show logos to a doll glass, but make sure it faces the camera! Place the kit's large-screen TV in back for screen clips.

Opera Diva

Dress your doll for an opening-night gala.

Operatic Dress

Create an Asian-inspired outfit for your doll's latest opera. To make it, ask an adult if you can cut a leg off an old pair of leggings. Put the gown on your doll, leaving the length long. Fold down the top edge. Slip a 10-inch ribbon around your doll's neck, and attach each end to the inside front with a Glue Dot. Wrap a longer ribbon around your doll's waist 2 times, and tie a big bow in back. Add the kit's butterfly to the ribbon with a dot.

Asian Accessories

For a hair accessory, attach stringed beads to 2 mini colored craft sticks. Give your doll an updo, and slip in the sticks. For a fan, cut the paper from a regular folding fan into a doll-sized fan. Glue a bead to the bottom. Slip a cord through the bead hole, and tie on colorful beads for danglers.

Background Curtains

For added drama, stand your singer in front of stage curtains. Position a 19½-by-23-inch frame vertically. For curtains, cut two 20-by-30-inch pieces of velvet. Ask an adult to tack each panel to the back edge of the frame at top, starting at the midpoint and working to the side. Then flip the curtains to the front, and tie them to the frame with gold cord. Lean the frame against a wall.

Baby Grand Piano

Bring in a piano player to accompany your doll's solos. Remove pages from a square photo album or binder. Cover 4 toilet-paper tubes and a 6-inch round craft stick with black duct tape. Use glue to attach the legs underneath the corners of the album, and the stick to hold open the album. Slip on the kit's keyboard. Use a gift box for a piano bench.

Celebrity Chef

Your chef can inspire other doll foodies on her cooking show.

Studio Kitchen

For a counter, attach 2 **wooden crates** (or cardboard boxes) side by side with **tape.** Cover the tops with **corkboard squares.** Use **Glue Dots** to attach **pretty paper** to the sides in front. Attach the **kit's cooking show sign** with a dot. For a stove top, tape together 2 **CD holders,** and use dots to cover them with silver **paper.** Pull out the kit's *Dazzling Desserts* cookbook, slip it on the **kit's book stand,** and place it on the counter. Decorate the counter with your doll's old cookware, dishes, or other odds and ends. Design desserts from **craft foam, beads,** and other **craft supplies.** Place the **movie camera** from page 15 in front of your doll's cooking set to capture her culinary skills.

THE
Sweet 'n' Small Chef SHOW
✫ American Girl®

Country Queen

Your country singer's star will rise when you put her on tour.

Keyboard

Tapping out a pretend tune will be a breeze with a portable piano. To make it, attach glitter paper to the outside of a shoebox lid using double-stick tape. Attach the kit's keyboard to the lid with Glue Dots. Ask an adult to cut two 9-inch legs from cardboard tubes. Roll the tubes in black duct tape, and attach them to the piano with the dots.

Acoustic Guitar

Give your doll a gorgeous guitar to pick or pluck. Pull out the kit's acoustic guitar and neck. Attach the neck to the guitar's body with Glue Dots. Use ribbon for a guitar strap.

Standing Mic

This classic mic makes crooning look oh, so cool. Wrap a thread spool with silver duct tape. Connect 2 silver unsharpened pencils together end to end with the tape. Push one end of the pencil pole into the spool hole, and slip a marker cap on the other end.

Popular Author

Send your bestselling writer on a booksigning tour.

Autograph Station

✋ Bring your doll to a bookstore to autograph copies of her latest novel. To make the store, ask an adult if you can attach the kit's mini bookshelf posters to a wall. Position your author behind a desk or box. For ink pens, cut straws into 1½-inch pieces, angling the ends into tips. Use a marker to color the pen nibs. Slip the pens into a plastic cap.

Novels & Stand

Make sure your doll has a stack of books for customers to purchase. Pull out the kit's novel covers and corrugated-cardboard pieces. Attach the covers to the cardboard with Glue Dots. Place a book face-forward on the kit's book stand, and stack the others nearby.

Star Reporter

Send your doll into the press pool to cover red-carpet events.

Reporter Tools

Shutterbugs need cameras—lots of cameras. Use Glue Dots to attach a ribbon strap to each of the kit's cameras. For a long lens, wrap a mini craft spool or wood wheel with black duct tape, and stick it to the camera lens with a dot. To add a flash, tape a mini LED light to the top of the camera. Pull out the kit's reporter's notebook for interviews.

Red Carpet

Cut a long rectangle from red wrapping paper for movie openings, award shows, or other special events. Invite your friends' dolls over to create a crowd-filled scene with adoring fans if you like.

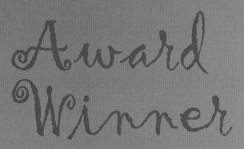

Award Winner

When your doll gives or receives an award, make sure she looks her best!

Designer Gowns

Nothing says "award show" like gorgeous gowns. To create one, ask an adult if you can cut a leg off an old pair of leggings. For each armhole, cut a 1-inch slit 1½ inches from the hemmed edge. Gently slip the dress on your doll, leaving the length long. Design options: Use Glue Dots to attach beaded trim to the neckline and hem. Or tie a scarf around the waist. Or decorate the front with rhinestone stickers. Or make a full skirt by using the dots to attach 5-by-12-inch strips of tulle to the back side of an 18-inch ribbon—leave 3 inches on each end to tie the skirt in back.

Fancy Podium

Create a pretty podium for handing out awards. Fill the bottom third of a clear plastic box with clear beads. Stack another box on top. Hide the box seams with ribbon and rhinestone sticker strips. For a mic, wrap a twist tie with black duct tape, and attach one end to the podium with a Glue Dot. Add a mini pom-pom to the other end. Adjust the mic to fit the speaker.

AG Star Awards

Hand out glamorous awards to the best performers of the year! To make one, cover a small wood block and wood star with nontoxic acrylic paint. Let dry. Attach the star to the block with a Glue Dot. Add one of the kit's award stickers to the block.

Celebrity Name

Give your doll a star name using one or both of your own initials.

**Find your first initial in list 1 and your last initial in list 2.
What's your doll's name to fame?**

List 1

A = Addison			N = Nina	
B = Blaine			O = Oriana	
C = Cameron			P = Portia	
D = Drucilla			Q = Quinn	
E = Eden			R = Reese	
F = Fleur			S = Skye	
G = Genevieve			T = Tuesday	
H = Hayden			U = Ula	
I = Isadora			V = Vivien	
J = Jade			W = Willow	
K = Kimmy			X = Xena	
L = Leilani			Y = Yvette	
M = Marcella			Z = Zafina	

List 2

A = Ashton			N = Nation	
B = Blakely			O = Olivier	
C = Cruise			P = Prince	
D = Darcy			Q = Quenby	
E = Evans			R = Rivers	
F = Fairfax			S = Summers	
G = Garnett			T = Truehart	
H = Hart			U = Underhill	
I = Ingram			V = Valentina	
J = James			W = Winters	
K = Knight			X = Xavier	
L = Locke			Y = Yardley	
M = Monroe			Z = Zander	

Let us know what kind of
star treatment you like
to give your doll.

Write to
Doll Star **Editor**
American Girl
8400 Fairway Place
Middleton, WI 53562

(Sorry, but photos can't be returned. All comments
and suggestions received by American Girl may be
used without compensation or acknowledgment.)

Here are some other American Girl books you might like:

❑ I read it.

❑ I read it.

❑ I read it.

❑ I read it.